Seedfolks

by
Paul Fleischman

Student Packet

Written by
Heather M. Marnan

Contains masters for:
- 2 Prereading Activities
- 7 Vocabulary Activities
- 1 Study Guide
- 2 Literary Analysis Activities
- 3 Character Analysis Activities
- 1 Comprehension Activity
- 1 Critical Thinking Activity
- 1 Writing Activity
- 3 Quizzes
- 1 Novel Test

PLUS Detailed Answer Key and Scoring Rubric

Note

The 2004 Harper Trophy paperback edition of the book, © 1997 by Paul Fleischman, was used to prepare this guide. The page references may differ in other editions. Novel ISBN: 978-0-06-447207-4

Please note: This novel deals with sensitive, mature issues. Parts may contain profanity, sexual references, and/or descriptions of violence. Please assess the appropriateness of this book for the age level and maturity of your students prior to reading and discussing it with them.

ISBN: 978-1-56137-079-5

Copyright infringement is a violation of l

© 2007 by Novel Units, Inc., Bulverde, Texas. All righ
be reproduced, translated, stored in a retrieval system,
(electronic, mechanical, photocopying, recording, or c
from ECS Learning Systems, Inc.

Photocopying of student worksheets by a classroom teacher at a non-profit school who has purchased this publication for his/her own class is permissible. Reproduction of any part of this publication for an entire school or for a school system, by for-profit institutions and tutoring centers, or for commercial sale is strictly prohibited.

Novel Units is a registered trademark of ECS Learning Systems, Inc.
Printed in the United States of America.

To order, contact your local school supply store, or—

PAPERBACKS - BMI BOUND BOOKS
TEACHER'S GUIDES - AUDIO-VISUALS
PO BOX 800 - DAYTON, N.J. 08810-0800
Toll Free Phone 1-800-222-8100
America's Finest Educational Book Distributor

www.bmionline.com

Name _____

Seedfolks
Activity #1 • Prereading
Use Before Reading

Getting the "Lay of the Land"

Directions: Prepare for reading by answering the following short-answer questions.

1. Who is the author?
   _____

2. What does the title suggest to you about the book?

   _____
   _____
   _____
   _____

3. When was the book first copyrighted?
   _____

4. How many pages are there in the book?
   _____

5. Thumb through the book. Read three pages—one from near the beginning, one from near the middle, and one from near the end. What predictions can you make about the book?

   _____
   _____
   _____
   _____

6. What does the cover suggest to you about the book?

   _____
   _____
   _____
   _____

© Novel Units, Inc.

Name _____

Seedfolks
Activity #2 • Prereading
Use Before Reading

Directions: On the lines below, write how each term might be dicussed in the novel. When you are done, freewrite for at least five minutes about each on a separate sheet of paper.

1. gardens _____
   _____

2. multicultural _____
   _____

3. community _____
   _____

4. first impressions _____
   _____

5. barriers _____
   _____

6. change _____
   _____

7. hope _____
   _____

8. racism _____
   _____

Name _____

Seedfolks
Activity #3 • Vocabulary
Kim–Wendell

altar	stern	incense	gnawing
vowed	thrive	vacant	lad
parole	wilted		

Directions: An analogy is a comparison of two similar objects or words. Look at the example below. Then, use the vocabulary words in the box to complete the analogies below.

Example: CASCADE is to FALL as SECURE is to SAFE.

1. DISCLOSURE is to SECRET as _____ is to INCARCERATION.

2. BARREN is to FRUITFUL as _____ is to UPRIGHT.

3. DESK is to SCHOOL as _____ is to CHURCH.

4. KITTEN is to CAT as _____ is to MAN.

5. INVITED is to WELCOMED as _____ is to PROMISED.

6. JOYFUL is to SMILE as _____ is to FROWN.

7. SUCCEED is to FAIL as _____ is to DIMINISH.

8. COLOGNE is to PERFUME as _____ is to POTPOURRI.

9. CUTTING is to KNIFE as _____ is to TEETH.

10. EMPTY is to LOADED as _____ is to OCCUPIED.

Name _____

Seedfolks
Activity #4 • Vocabulary
Gonzalo–Leona

Vocabulary World Map

equation	*bodega*	pueblo	gestures
trowel	troughs	citizens	maggots
receptionist			

Directions: Complete the word map for al least 5 of the above vocabulary words.

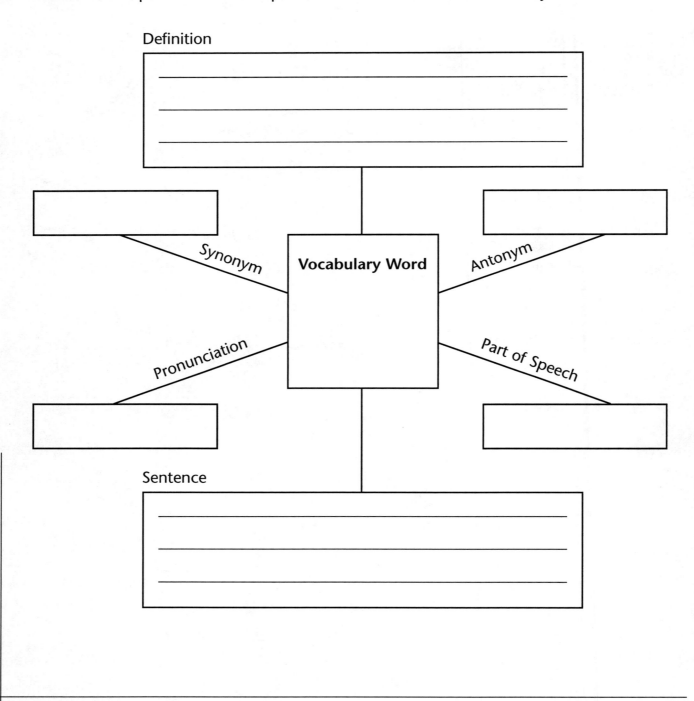

Name _____

Seedfolks
Activity #5 • Vocabulary
Sam–Virgil

Vocabulary Flashcard

Directions: Create flashcards with the word on one side and definition on the other. Working with a partner, quiz each other for five to ten minutes. Then switch to a new partner, and quiz each other for another five to ten minutes.

1. herring: a fish that lives in cold regions
2. occupation: a job or career
3. pacifism: opposition to war or violence as a means of settling disputes
4. compromised: settled a dispute; made an agreement
5. spigot: a faucet to regulate the flow of water
6. crowning: implying splendor, honor, or achievement
7. pecking: striking or biting with beak or teeth
8. plantation: a large group of plants under cultivation
9. myths: traditional stories, usually fictional
10. goddess: a female god; a woman who is adored

Name _____

Seedfolks
Activity #6 • Vocabulary
Sae Young–Curtis

alterations	interrupt	spout	pecs
deeds	blight	fertilizer	sharecropper
billard			

Directions: Create nine short-answer questions about this section, and use a synonym of at least one vocabulary word in each question you create. Write your questions on the lines below. Switch with a partner and answer.

1. _____

2. _____

3. _____

4. _____

5. _____

6. _____

7. _____

8. _____

9. _____

Name _____

Seedfolks
Activity #7 • Vocabulary
Nora–Maricela

Vocabulary Sentence Sets

prams	gales	dignified	obliged
haphazard	domestic	entranced	tremolo
furrowed	pantomime	notion	chard
decorum	disgrace		

Directions: Write the vocabulary words from the list above on the numbered lines below.

1. _____ 2. _____
3. _____ 4. _____
5. _____ 6. _____
7. _____ 8. _____
9. _____ 10. _____
11. _____ 12. _____
13. _____ 14. _____

On a separate sheet of paper, use each of the following sets of words in an original sentence. Your sentences should show that you know the meanings of the vocabulary words as they are used in the story.

Sentence 1: words 8 and 4
Sentence 2: words 9 and 3
Sentence 3: words 1 and 10
Sentence 4: words 11 and 7
Sentence 5: words 2 and 13
Sentence 6: words 3 and 6
Sentence 7: words 12 and 4
Sentence 8: words 14 and 9
Sentence 9: words 5 and 2
Sentence 10: words 7 and 6

Name _____

Seedfolks
Activity #8 • Vocabulary
Amir–Florence

| vast | foes | eerie | spit |
| homesteaded | arthritis | sampler | idle |

Directions: Pretend you are a reporter for a Cleveland newspaper. Write an article about how the garden has affected community relations. Include quotes from characters working in the garden, and use all of the vocabulary words listed above in your article. Continue the article on a separate sheet of paper if necessary.

Gibb Street News

Wednesday, October 2 • Section A, Page 1

_____
_____
_____
_____
_____
_____
_____
_____
_____
_____
_____
_____
_____
_____
_____
_____

Name _____

Seedfolks
Activity #9 • Vocabulary
From Seed to Seedfolks

Vocabulary Chart

affliction	serendipity	tabloid	camaraderie
monologues	aversion	presaging	baron
propagation	vigilance	aria	invective
pillaging	waived	solace	altruism
potent			

Directions: Write each vocabulary word in the left-hand column of the chart. Complete the chart by placing a check mark in the column that best describes your familiarity with each word. Working with a partner, find and read the line where each word appears in the story. Find the meaning of each word in the dictionary. Together with your partner, choose ten of the words checked in the last column. On a separate sheet of paper, use each of those words in a sentence.

Vocabulary Word	I Can Define	I Have Seen/Heard	New Word For Me

Name _____

Seedfolks
Study Guide

Kim–Wendell
1. For what does Kim wish as she stands at her family's altar?
2. What is Kim's nationality?
3. Why is Kim sad when she thinks of her father?
4. Why does Kim believe her father will be proud of her for planting the lima bean seeds?
5. What does Ana see from her apartment window?
6. What does Ana assume about the girl she sees in the vacant lot?
7. What does Ana do when the girl leaves?
8. Why do you suppose Ana buys binoculars for herself?
9. Why does Wendell dislike phone calls?
10. What does Ana want Wendell to do?
11. Why do you suppose Kim is afraid when she sees Wendell? Is her fear rational?
12. After seeing Kim, what does Wendell decide to do?

Gonzalo–Leona
1. Why does Gonzalo believe his father got younger after moving to the United States?
2. How does Gonzalo come to care for his Tío Juan?
3. Whom is Tío Juan trying to talk to in the vacant lot? How do you know?
4. Why do you suppose Gonzalo hopes no one will see him in the vacant lot?
5. How does planting the seeds help Tío Juan "[change]... back into a man"?
6. Explain the irony of the medical advice given to Leona's grandmother.
7. Why do you suppose Leona decides to plant goldenrod in the vacant lot?
8. What does Leona see as the main problem with the vacant lot? How does she plan to resolve the problem?
9. What does Leona realize as she makes each phone call about the vacant lot?
10. Do you think Leona makes a good decision when she brings the trash bag to the health department? Why or why not?

Name _____

Seedfolks
Study Guide
page 2

Sam–Virgil

1. What does Sam see happening at the vacant lot? What does this tell you?
2. How do you feel about Sam wanting to participate in the community garden but hiring children to do most of the work?
3. What problems does Sam see in the garden?
4. What does Virgil find while digging in the garden? Why do you suppose he keeps it?
5. What does Virgil's father plan to do with their spot in the garden?
6. How do you feel about Virgil's father lying to Miss Fleck? Do you think it was her business to question the size of their garden?
7. What happens to the lettuce Virgil and his father plant? How does this make each of them feel?
8. How does Virgil attempt to help the situation?

Sae Young–Curtis

1. What happens to Sae Young at her dry cleaning shop?
2. How does Sae Young react following the incident? Do you think her reaction is rational? Why or why not?
3. What effect does the garden have on Sae Young?
4. How does Sam's contest unite people?
5. How does Sae Young contribute to the winning idea for bringing water to the garden? How does this make her feel?
6. What does Curtis think of himself?
7. Why does Curtis no longer have a girlfriend?
8. How does Curtis intend to make Lateesha notice and like him again? What does he do?
9. How does Curtis protect his tomato plants after he discovers some of the tomatoes are missing?
10. Do you think Curtis' plan to win Lateesha's affection will work? Why or why not?

Nora–Maricela

1. What is Nora's occupation?
2. How does Mr. Myles surprise Nora during one of their walks? Why does this surprise her?
3. What does Nora do for Mr. Myles after they visit the garden?
4. How does Mr. Myles respond to being in the garden?

5. What does Nora witness happening to the neighborhood as a result of visiting the garden?
6. Briefly describe Maricela and her current situation.
7. Why does Maricela visit the community garden?
8. How does Maricela feel about visiting the garden?
9. To whom does Maricela finally speak? Why do you suppose she feels comfortable talking to this person?
10. What does Maricela learn? How does this make her feel?

Amir–Florence
1. How does Amir compare and contrast India and America?
2. What does Amir believe to be the garden's greatest effect?
3. How do Amir's thoughts and feelings about Polish people change after visiting the garden?
4. In what way does the garden help to banish suspicions about Royce?
5. Does Amir enjoy the camaraderie created by the garden? How does he explain his feelings?
6. To whom does Amir speak at the harvest festival? How does this person explain her previous bad behavior? Do you think her explanation is fair?
7. How does Florence compare her ancestors to the people in the garden?
8. Why can't Florence plant anything in the garden? How does she participate instead?
9. Why does Florence begin to worry about the garden?
10. What fills Florence with hope again?

Afterword: From Seed to Seedfolks
1. How did the author get the idea to write *Seedfolks*?
2. How does the author compare writers to gardeners?
3. What characteristics does the author feel he has inherited from his father? his mother?
4. What does the author believe is the hardest part of writing a book?
5. How did the author create the characters in *Seedfolks*?
6. Why is the author a proponent of community gardens?

Name _____

Seedfolks
Activity #10 • Literary Analysis
Use During Reading

Story Map

Directions: Complete the story map below using details you have learned while reading *Seedfolks*.

Title

Setting, Characters, Problem

Beginning

Important Events

Climax (Turning Point)

End

© Novel Units, Inc.

Seedfolks
Name _____

Activity #11 • Character Analysis
Use During and After Reading

Understanding Values

Values represent people's beliefs about what is important, good, or worthwhile. For example, most families value spending time together.

Directions: Think about Kim, Leona, Sam, Sae Young, Curtis, and Florence and the values they exhibit. What do they value? What beliefs do they have about what is important, good, or worthwhile? On the chart below, list each character's three most important values, from most important to least. Be prepared to share your lists during a class discussion.

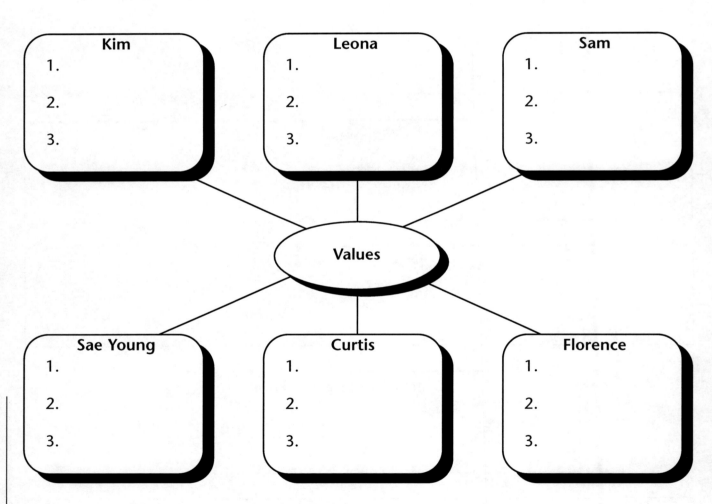

After you have finished the chart and participated in the class discussion, think about which character seems to have values most like your own. Write a paragraph that explains why you chose this character.

Name _____

Seedfolks
Activity #12 • Critical Thinking
Use After Reading

Attribute Web

Directions: On each long spoke surrounding the oval, write the name of a character who contributes to the garden community. On each short spoke, write a word or phrase that describes how the character contributes.

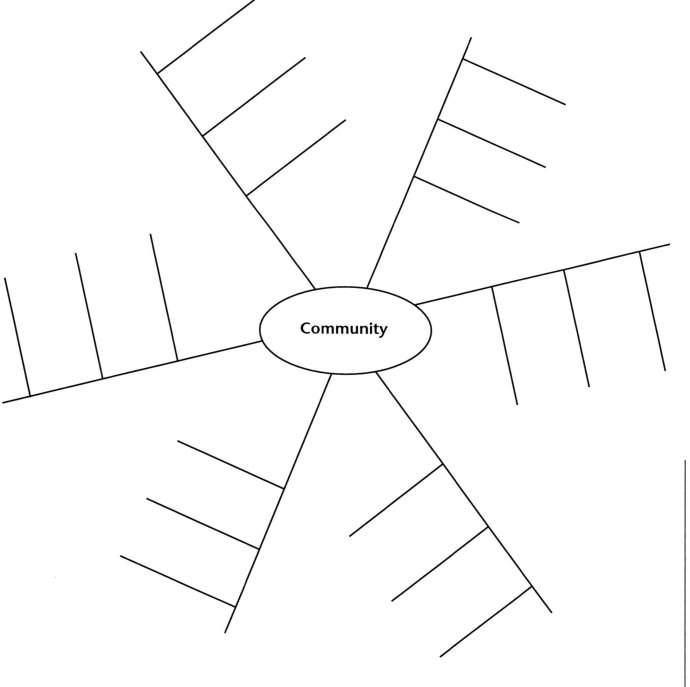

© Novel Units, Inc. 17

Name _____

Seedfolks
Activity #13 • Character Analysis
Use After Reading

Character Analysis Blocks

Directions: Select a character from the book to describe using the blocks below.

	Who is the character?		
	What does the character do?	Why does s/he do it?	
What, if anything, is significant about the character's name?	What is the nature of this character's actions? (reactive, active, important, consequential, secondary)	What is the significance of the book's time and place to the character?	
What is unusual or important about the character?	How does the character change in the story?	Does the character remind you of another character from another book? Who?	Do you know anyone similar to this character?

Name _____

Seedfolks
Activity #14 • Character Analysis
Use After Reading

Character Web

Directions: Complete the attribute web by filling in information specific to a character in the book.

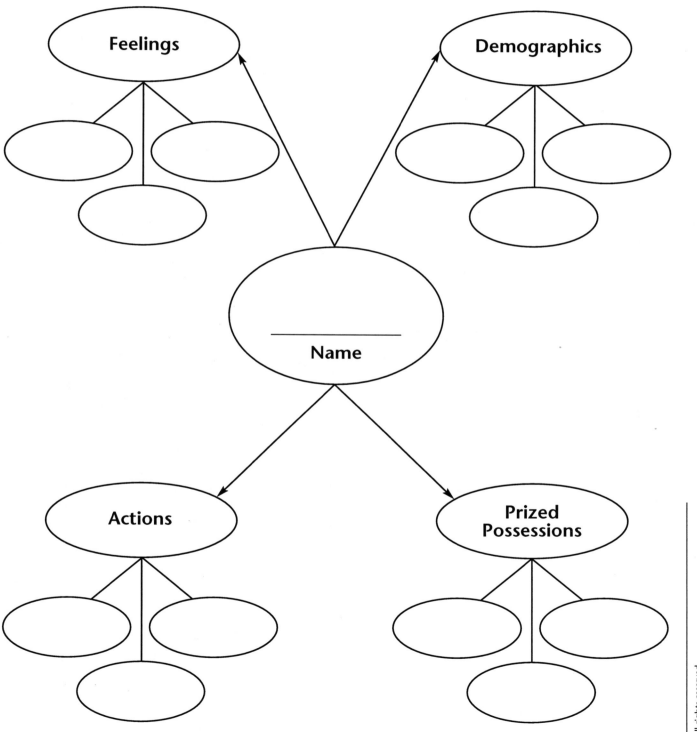

© Novel Units, Inc. | 19

Name _____

Seedfolks
Activity #15 • Literary Analysis
Use After Reading

Metaphors and Similes

A **metaphor** is a comparison between two unlike objects. For example, "he was a human tree." A **simile** is a comparison between two unlike objects that uses the words *like* or *as*. For example, "the color of her eyes was like the cloudless sky."

Directions: Complete the chart below by listing metaphors and similes from the novel, as well as the page numbers on which they are found. Identify metaphors with an "M" and similes with an "S." Translate the comparisons in your own words, and then list the objects being compared.

Metaphors/Similes	Ideas/Objects Being Compared
1. Translation:	
2. Translation:	
3. Translation:	

Name _____

Seedfolks
Activity #16 • Comprehension
Use After Reading

Directions: Choose two characters from the novel. Using the Venn diagram below, compare and contrast the characters.

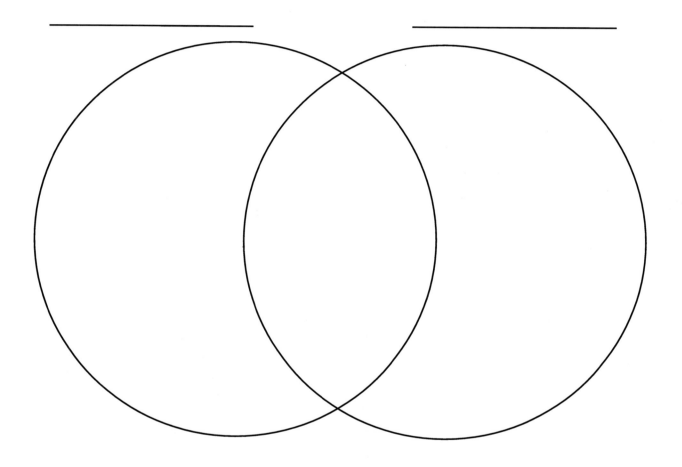

Name _____

Seedfolks
Activity #17 • Writing
Use After Reading

Directions: Think of a place in your neighborhood where a community garden could be started. Who would use the garden? How would it benefit the community? What issues might need to be resolved? On the lines below, write a "Letter to the Editor" of a local newspaper convincing the community that such a garden would be a good, or bad, idea. Use a separate sheet of paper if you need more room.

_____
_____
_____
_____
_____
_____
_____
_____
_____
_____
_____
_____
_____
_____
_____
_____
_____
_____
_____
_____
_____
_____

Name _____

Seedfolks
Quiz #1
Kim–Leona

Short Answer: Write a brief answer to each of the following questions. Use a separate sheet of paper if necessary.

1. Why does Kim enter the vacant lot?

2. Why is Kim sad when she thinks of her father?

3. How does Kim hope to have her father notice her?

4. How has the neighborhood changed since Ana moved there?

5. What does Ana believe Kim is doing in the vacant lot? Why does she think this?

6. Whom does Ana call to help her save Kim's plants?

7. Why does Wendell dislike receiving phone calls?

8. What does Wendell do to Kim's plants?

9. How do Kim's plants and the vacant lot give Wendell hope?

10. What is "Garcia's Equation"?

11. Why does Gonzalo think that his father and uncle have gotten younger since arriving in the United States?

12. What effect does planting the seeds have on Gonzalo's uncle?

13. How does Leona intend to honor her grandmother?

14. What bothers Leona most about the vacant lot?

15. To whom does Leona speak about the vacant lot? What are the results?

Name _____

Seedfolks
Quiz #2
Sam–Curtis

A. Identification: In one or two sentences, describe how each of the following are important to the story. Use a separate sheet of paper if necessary.

1. paradise

2. locket

3. lettuce

4. dry cleaning shop

5. funnels

6. chicken wire

B. True/False: Mark each statement T if it is true and F if it is false.

____ 7. Sam is a Jewish man who likes to cause conflict.

____ 8. Sam hosts a contest for the children to solve the garden's water problem.

____ 9. Virgil and his father plan to use the garden for profit.

____ 10. Miss Fleck is pleased with Virgil and his father when she sees their patch of garden.

____ 11. Sae Young is robbed in her dry cleaning shop by a man carrying a knife.

____ 12. Sae Young avoids the people in the garden and chooses to work alone.

____ 13. Sam asks Sae Young to provide funnels for the water cans in the garden.

____ 14. Curtis plants tomatoes in the garden so Lateesha will notice him.

____ 15. Curtis hires a teenager named Royce to fertilize and water his plants.

____ 16. Lateesha watches Curtis in the garden, but does not join him.

Name _____

Seedfolks
Quiz #3
Nora–Florence

A. Multiple Choice: Choose the BEST answer to each of the following questions.

___ 1. Nora tries to take Mr. Myles for a daily

    A. cup of coffee

    B. movie

    C. picnic

    D. walk

___ 2. Nora and Mr. Myles plant flowers in the garden using

    A. metal troughs

    B. barrels filled with dirt

    C. old coffee cans filled with sand

    D. soup cans with the tops cut out

___ 3. Nora and Mr. Myles meet the other people in the garden

    A. because Mr. Myles introduces himself

    B. when the neighborhood has a produce sale

    C. after a rainstorm forces them to find shelter

    D. after Nora asks each person for a gardening tip

___ 4. Maricela dislikes herself because she is

    A. pregnant

    B. just like everyone else

    C. fighting with her parents

    D. unable to graduate due to poor grades

___ 5. Why does Maricela visit the garden?

    A. Her school is doing a science project in the garden.

    B. Her friends invite her to plant vegetables in the garden.

    C. Her support group goes to the garden as part of the program.

    D. Her parents want her to learn to plant flowers at her own house.

© Novel Units, Inc.

Name _____

Seedfolks
Quiz #3
page 2

___ 6. Maricela feels some comfort after speaking with

   A. Leona

   B. Nora

   C. Sam

   D. Wendell

___ 7. What does Amir think about Americans?

   A. They are cruel.

   B. They are insincere.

   C. They are suspicious.

   D. They are unintelligent.

___ 8. Amir's own stereotypical beliefs are challenged when he

   A. speaks with a Polish woman

   B. observes Royce's actions in the garden

   C. participates in a Mexican family's barbecue

   D. all of the above

___ 9. Florence has many fond memories of her home

   A. in the city

   B. in the country

   C. near the seashore

   D. near the mountains

___10. Florence worries that the garden will

   A. be forgotten in the spring

   B. cause trouble for the neighborhood

   C. attract homeless people to the neighborhood

   D. become too crowded when the gardeners return

Name _____

Seedfolks
Quiz #3
page 3

B. Quotations: Match the following quotations to the correct character from the novel.

| a. Amir | b. Maricela | c. Florence | d. Nora |

___11. "It had been such a wonderful change to see people making something for themselves...."

___12. "We, like our seeds, were now planted in the garden."

___13. "I was just a watcher, but I was proud of the garden, as if it were mine."

___14. "But the garden's greatest benefit...was not relief to the eyes, but to make the eyes see our neighbors."

___15. "It seemed like I could actually see the leaves and flowers growing and changing."

___16. "We mustn't stop living before our time."

Name _____

Seedfolks
Novel Test

A. Identification: Match each character with his/her correct description.

____ 1. Kim

____ 2. Ana

____ 3. Wendell

____ 4. Gonzalo

____ 5. Leona

____ 6. Sam

____ 7. Virgil

____ 8. Sae Young

____ 9. Curtis

____ 10. Nora

____ 11. Maricela

____ 12. Amir

____ 13. Florence

a. frightened Korean woman; feels safe in the garden
b. young man who plants tomatoes in the garden for an ex-girlfriend
c. Jewish man who hosts a gardening contest for children
d. young girl who hopes her father notices her in the garden
e. concerned woman who demands that the vacant lot be cleaned up
f. depressed teenage girl; feels happy for a brief moment in the garden
g. British nurse who helps her patient plant flowers in the garden
h. nosy woman; destroys Kim's bean plants
i. Indian man whose own stereotypical beliefs are challenged by the people in the garden
j. middle-aged man who helps save Kim's bean plants
k. young man in charge of helping his uncle function in America
l. middle-aged woman who hopes the garden continues in the spring
m. young man who helps his father plant lettuce for profit

Name _____

Seedfolks
Novel Test
page 2

B. Short Answer: Write a brief answer to each of the following questions. Use a separate sheet of paper if necessary.

14. What saddens Kim the most about her father's death?

15. How does Ana rationalize her suspicions about Kim's activity in the garden?

16. For whom is Gonzalo responsible? Why must he take care of this person?

17. Why does Leona go to the health department? How does she accomplish her goal?

18. How does Sam attempt to promote peace and unity among people?

19. What is the result of Virgil and his father's plan to make money? Why is Virgil angry with his father?

20. How does the garden help Sae Young?

21. Why does Curtis enlist Royce's help with his tomato plants?

22. What does Nora believe about life? Why does she believe this?

23. What does Maricela think about in the garden that brings her a brief moment of hope?

24. How does Amir feel in the garden? How do others feel about him?

25. What is Florence's greatest fear about the garden? What happens to subdue her fear?

© Novel Units, Inc.

Name _____

Seedfolks
Novel Test
page 3

Character Web

C. Character Analysis: Choose a character from the novel, and complete the chart below.

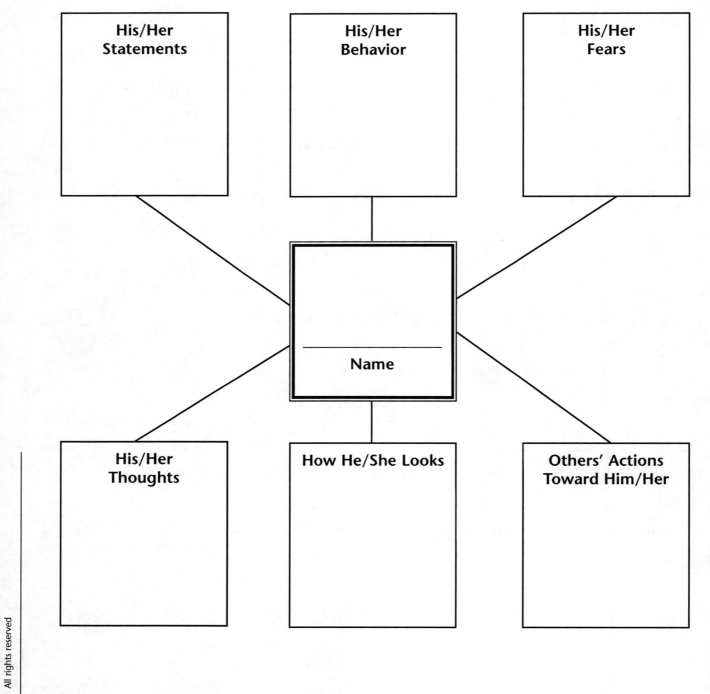

Name _____

Seedfolks
Novel Test
page 4

D. Essay: Write a well-developed essay for one of the following prompts. Use evidence from the novel to support your response.

I. Examine the issue of "nature vs. nurture" in the novel. Which has the greatest effect on the garden? On the characters? Who or what is the most affected by nature? By nurture? Cite specific examples from the novel to support your response.

II. Throughout the novel, Kim is referred to with different designations [i.e., Chinese (Wendell), Vietnamese (Sae Young), Oriental (Florence)]. State which designation is correct and the possible reasons why that particular character was correct. Analyze the universality of this type of mistake when discussing people of different nationalities.

Answer Key

Activity #1: 1. Paul Fleischman 2. Answers will vary. 3. 1997 4. 102 pages 5. Answers will vary. 6. Answers will vary. Suggestion: People of different ages and cultures will be planting the seeds, each with his/her own specific story.

Activity #2: Answers will vary.

Activity #3: 1. PAROLE 2. WILTED 3. ALTAR 4. LAD 5. VOWED 6. STERN 7. THRIVE 8. INCENSE 9. GNAWING 10. VACANT

Activity #4: Example: Vocabulary Word—trowel; Synonym—spade, shovel; Antonym—rake; Pronunciation—trau(-ə)l; Part of Speech—noun; Definition—a small, short-handled shovel used to dig in gardens, flowerbeds, and other confined spaces; Sentence—She used a trowel to delicately dig the holes where she would plant her tulip bulbs.

Activity #5: Students will create and use flashcards.

Activity #6: Students will create short-answer questions and exchange.

Activities #7–#9: Answers will vary.

Study Guide

Kim–Wendell: 1. She wishes her father's eyes would move within his photograph and look at her. 2. Vietnamese 3. He died before she was born, and she does not have any memories of him, nor him of her. 4. Her father was a farmer, and he will see her plants grow. 5. Many people of different cultures come and go in the neighborhood. 6. that she is acting suspiciously, doing something wrong because she is young, and/or burying something illegal 7. Ana digs up the lima bean seeds. 8. Answers will vary. Suggestions: so that she will not make another mistake when watching people, so she can watch the seeds in the garden, etc. 9. He always gets bad news when the phone rings. 10. water Kim's bean seeds 11. Answers will vary. 12. He decides to claim a part of the vacant lot for his own use because it is something in his life he can change for the better.

Gonzalo–Leona: 1. Since he does not know English, Gonzalo's father asks his son to do everything for him. Gonzalo feels as though he is taking care of his father, like a parent with a child. 2. His uncle cannot speak English and wanders out into the neighborhood. 3. Wendell; Gonzalo says the man is a school janitor. 4. Answers will vary. 5. Tío Juan knows how to tend a garden, and planting the seeds gives him something to do that he is good at. 6. Granny outlives all of the doctors who disapprove of her lifestyle. 7. in memory of her grandmother 8. The lot is full of trash, and the city will not clean it up; She calls several agencies until she finds the one responsible for the lot. 9. She needs to talk to someone in person in order to get noticed. 10. Answers will vary.

Sam–Virgil: 1. Men are clearing the lot. Leona succeeded in her task. 2. Answers will vary. 3. no way to get water nearby, groups of people divided within the garden, garbage everywhere, people arguing 4. a locket with a girl's picture inside; Answers will vary. 5. plant lettuce to sell to restaurants 6. Answers will vary. 7. It comes up crooked, wilts, and bugs eat the leaves; Virgil's father is extremely upset, and Virgil is angry. 8. He implores the girl in the locket picture to save their lettuce.

Sae Young–Curtis: 1. She was robbed at gunpoint, and the thief attacked her. 2. She is afraid of people and afraid to leave her apartment; Answers will vary. 3. She feels happy to be around people again. She likes the sound of people working and talking and is not afraid when someone speaks to her. 4. Children give ideas on bringing water to the garden, and everyone claps for the winning idea. Some also give money to buy garbage cans for collecting the water. 5. She buys funnels to make it easier to pour water; She feels happy when people use the funnels, like she belongs in the garden.

6. He thinks he is good-looking, with a muscular body. 7. His girlfriend, Lateesha, caught him with another girl. 8. He wants to grow tomato plants because Lateesha loves to eat tomatoes; He plants the tomatoes and tends to them every day, hoping Lateesha will look out her window and see the tomatoes growing. 9. He puts chicken wire over them. When that does not work, he enlists the help of an intimidating black boy to watch over the plants at night. During the day, he puts a sign near the plants that reads "Lateesha's Tomatoes." 10. Answers will vary.

Nora–Maricela: 1. She is a nurse for an elderly man, Mr. Myles, who suffered a stroke that has left him unable to speak. 2. He raises his arm, signaling her to stop in front of the community garden; he almost never responds to the world around him during their walks. 3. She brings Mr. Myles to the garden and fills a large barrel with soil so that he can plant flowers from his wheelchair. 4. He is excited and happy. Nora sees him regain some of his spirit and vitality when he is tending to his plants. 5. People are unified through their participation in the garden. No matter what the culture or language, everyone has a common bond because of the garden. 6. She is a 16-year-old Mexican girl. She is pregnant and very unhappy with her life, even wishing that she and her unborn child were dead. 7. She is part of a support group for pregnant teens, and the director brings the girls to the garden as part of the program. 8. Maricela does not like being in the garden. She dislikes the people there, and she resents any interaction with them. She is generally miserable, and being in the garden only reminds her that she is different from others. 9. Leona; Answers will vary. 10. Everyone is a part of nature's systems, and it is an honor to be part of such a system; Maricela begins to feel more at ease, and she stops thinking about hurting/killing her child.

Amir–Florence: 1. He says that both India and America have many large cities; however, people in India are friendly and enjoy getting to know each other, while in America they are unfriendly. 2. He thinks the garden allows people who might not otherwise interact to be friendly and helpful to one another. 3. He once believed the stereotypes about Polish people, but after meeting a Polish woman in the garden and learning her history, he realizes that what he previously believed was both incorrect and irrelevant. 4. Before becoming a part of the garden, Royce frightened people and filled them with suspicion. Now, he is well-known and well-liked because people have gotten to know him. 5. Yes; He says everyone "felt the…spirit enter" them. 6. a woman who had spoken badly about him in his store; She insists she didn't know it was him, insinuating that had she known him personally at the time she never would have done such a thing; Answers will vary. 7. She refers to the garden visitors as "seedfolks" because they began the garden from nothing, just as her father called her ancestors "seedfolks" because they started a family after being freed from slavery. 8. She has arthritis in her hands; She walks by the garden almost every day and keeps people from bothering it. 9. The seasons change, and no one is coming back to the garden because fall and winter make it impossible. 10. She sees Kim planting lima beans in the garden and notices another person watching, just as she is watching.

Afterword: From Seed to Seedfolks: 1. by reading an article about a therapist using gardening to help her patients 2. He believes both writers and gardeners are self-taught and self-sufficient. 3. the ability to write; the desire to help others 4. determining the title of the book 5. Some had been created years before, but never put into a book. Others came from people he read about, and still others were based on his own personality. 6. Gardens are a part of nature, and he believes that nature has a healing effect. Community gardens bring people together, and "heal" all of their prejudices and past hurts.

Note: Answers to Activities #10–#17 will vary. Suggested answers are given where appropriate.

Activity #10: Title: *Seedfolks*; all other answers will vary.

Activity #11: Suggestions: Kim: family, hard work, diligence; Leona: grandmother, cleanliness, accountability; Sam: peace, tolerance, unity; Sae Young: freedom, personal safety, feeling like she belongs; Curtis: physical appearances, redemption, Lateesha's opinion; Florence: memories of home, being active, springtime

Activity #12: Suggestion: Long Spoke—Sam; Short Spokes—friendliness, support, water contest

Activity #13–#17: Answers will vary.

Quiz #1: 1. She wants to plant some lima bean seeds in the vacant lot. 2. Her father died before she was born, and she does not have any memories of him to hold onto. 3. Since her father was a farmer, Kim hopes that his spirit will see her growing the lima beans and he will be proud of her. 4. Many different people of varying races and cultures have moved in and out of the neighborhood. 5. burying something/doing something illegal; She assumes this because Kim is young. 6. Wendell 7. Phone calls always seem to bring him bad news. 8. He makes a circle in the dirt around each plant so that the rain will collect around the plant. 9. He feels he can change something for the better by planting seeds there. 10. "The older you are, the younger you get when you move to the United States"—Gonzalo made it up after witnessing his family's transition to America. 11. Neither one can speak English and they have to ask others for help with even the most basic tasks. 12. His uncle is happy and focused; he does not need help while in the vacant lot with his seeds. 13. She plans to plant goldenrod, her grandmother's "medicine" of choice, in the vacant lot. 14. the garbage that no one sees fit to clean up 15. the Public Health Department; After bringing in a bag of trash from the vacant lot, Leona gets noticed and her cleaning requests are granted.

Quiz #2: A. 1. Sam thinks the garden in the vacant lot is like paradise because it brings people together. However, like the paradise of the Garden of Eden, this garden can also crumble because of division and hatred. 2. Virgil finds a locket in the garden and asks the girl whose picture is inside for help when their crop fails. 3. Virgil and his father plant lettuce in hopes of selling it and making money. 4. Sae Young is robbed and attacked in her dry cleaning shop, causing her to be afraid all of the time. 5. Sae Young provides funnels to help irrigate the garden. When people use these funnels, Sae Young feels like she belongs and is not afraid. 6. Curtis puts chicken wire around his tomato plants for Lateesha, hoping to keep out those who are stealing his tomatoes; it may signify the beginning of suspicion in the garden. **B.** 7. F 8. T 9. T 10. F 11. F 12. F 13. F 14. T 15. F 16. T

Quiz #3: A. 1. D 2. B 3. C 4. A 5. C 6. A 7. C 8. D 9. B 10. A **B.** 11. c (p.85) 12. d (p.65) 13. c (p. 84) 14. a (p. 74) 15. b (p. 72) 16. d (pp. 59–60)

Novel Test: A. 1. d 2. h 3. j 4. k 5. e 6. c 7. m 8. a 9. b 10. g 11. f 12. i 13. l **B.** 14. Since he died before she was born, Kim has no memories of her father and he has none of her. 15. Kim is "hiding" and "looking around suspiciously," and since she is young, she must be doing something illegal. 16. his uncle; Since moving to America, Gonzalo's uncle has been unable to function normally because he does not speak English. 17. She wants the city to clean up the vacant lot; She brings a bag of trash from the vacant lot into the office, and she is met with promptly after that. 18. He smiles at people, especially minorities. He forces people to look him in his eyes and he initiates conversation. 19. Their lettuce plants grow crooked, the leaves wilt, and insects begin eating the plants. The plants die, and their hope for profit is gone; Virgil is angry because he won't get the new bike he had been promised. 20. After being attacked at gunpoint, Sae Young was afraid of leaving her house and of people in general. When she visits the garden, she feels safe and happy. 21. People on the street are stealing his tomatoes, so Curtis asks Royce to stand guard at night. 22. People should not stop living just because they grow old; She witnessed her father lying around and doing nothing once he got older. 23. She reflects on Leona's statements about how she (Maricela) is part of nature's system and should be proud of that. 24. He feels connected to the other people there, no matter their differences; The people in the garden feel the same, as evidenced by the woman's statement about why she was rude to Amir in his store. 25. She fears no one will return to replant the garden; She sees Kim in the garden and a fellow onlooker in his home. **C.** Suggestion: Name—Leona; Her Statements—"Looking at [the trash], I knew this wasn't a job for no wheelbarrow. This was a job for the telephone." "I had to make myself real to 'em." Her Behavior—concerned, committed, tenacious, clever; Her Fears—N/A; Her Thoughts—determines most effective way to get vacant lot cleaned up, wonders how to get prompt action; How She Looks—30-something black woman; Others' Actions Toward Her—Officials ignore her until she brings the bag of trash to the health department. She is noticed very quickly afterward. **D.** Answers will vary. Refer to the scoring rubric on page 36 of this guide.

Linking Novel Units® Student Packets to National and State Reading Assessments

During the past several years, an increasing number of students have faced some form of state-mandated competency testing in reading. Many states now administer state-developed assessments to measure the skills and knowledge emphasized in their particular reading curriculum. This Novel Units® guide includes open-ended comprehension questions that correlate with state-mandated reading assessments. The rubric below provides important information for evaluating responses to open-ended comprehension questions. Teachers may also use scoring rubrics provided for their own state's competency test.

Scoring Rubric for Open-Ended Items

3-Exemplary	Thorough, complete ideas/information Clear organization throughout Logical reasoning/conclusions Thorough understanding of reading task Accurate, complete response
2-Sufficient	Many relevant ideas/pieces of information Clear organization throughout most of response Minor problems in logical reasoning/conclusions General understanding of reading task Generally accurate and complete response
1-Partially Sufficient	Minimally relevant ideas/information Obvious gaps in organization Obvious problems in logical reasoning/conclusions Minimal understanding of reading task Inaccuracies/incomplete response
0-Insufficient	Irrelevant ideas/information No coherent organization Major problems in logical reasoning/conclusions Little or no understanding of reading task Generally inaccurate/incomplete response